Dog

Chinese

Horoscope

2025

By
IChingHunFùyǒu FengShuisu

Table of Contents

Introduce

The character of people born in the year of the DOG

People born in the Year of the Dog are good people who are honest, trustworthy, and considerate when others ask for assistance. You are sincere, open, honest, and tenacious. But he is never selfish; he always thinks of others first. The heart is filled with love and virtue, and it is ready to fight for the rights of both oneself and others. It is usually very gentle when it comes to manners. However, it is concealed by a distorted ax-like character. You are a loyal companion despite being angry and irritable with your friends. Be sincere and do not betray those who have placed their trust in you.

Strength:

You are always up to date on events, have a keen understanding of the situation, and never abandon your friends in difficult times.

Weaknesses:
You are overly concerned with the affairs of others, which makes it easy for you to get into trouble.

Love:
People born in the Year of the Dog are unafraid of silent love. Maybe we've known each other for almost a year. Nobody knows at work. The secret is broken when you become involved with someone until someone secretly sees you. People born this year are quiet people who enjoy solitude but have a quiet demeanor. I'll tell you that love affairs will not be easy on your love story. People born in the Year of the Dog experience chaos as well. This type of lust results from being careless and not being afraid to sacrifice yourself. I just want to have fun sometimes, but withdrawing is also difficult.
When there is a lover as a person, the people of the Year of the Dog will stop all flirting and immediately turn to love and love.

Suitable Career:

People born in the Year of the Dog are classified as earth elemental. As a result, suitable occupations are primarily related to land or land, such as real estate work, land trades, photography, and welding. Selling electrical appliances, restaurants, beauty salons, mining - stone. Agriculture in all forms or doing business with agricultural products as a component, such as baking, processed fruit, ceramics, and pottery. Consultants in construction materials, banking, finance, and securities Selling paper machines to pay homage to the gods, performing government service, and so on.

Year of the DOG (Wood) | (1946) & (2006)

"The Dog take a nap" is a person born in the year of the DOG at the age of 79 years (1946) and 19 years (2006)

Overview

For senior horoscopes in this age group, this year, the horoscope is unstable. In the first half of the year, you should be careful about health and safety problems in the home. When traveling, you should have someone to take care of you closely. In addition, you should be careful of losing your property. What is very important this year is that you should be more strict about your health and not get involved or interfere in your children's affairs. This will make your family happy and your children will respect and love you. Doing good deeds will make your life peaceful and smooth in the end.

For teenagers in this age group, this year is another year that every activity requires caution. You cannot be hasty. Look clearly. Find complete knowledge before doing it. In addition, you should always build and strengthen your relationships with people around you. Be careful of gathering with friends, as you may be led to do bad things and cause trouble for others. Because the influence of the evil star Kua Hu often causes arguments and accidents, going to the police station or court, which can easily lead to lawsuits. The influence of the star Ham Tee (the star of love) causes the horoscope to often be led to vices like to travel and seek pleasure, so there may be problems. Therefore, if you can avoid immoral places, it will be good. You must also know how to reject friends who tend to lead you to vices. Be careful not to have arguments and get into misfortune from things you did not do, but you must share the responsibility for it. In addition, you must be careful of accidents and dangers from driving on the road.

Career and Business

For teenagers, even though this year many bad stars are staring at you, causing obstacles to hinder your career and education, if you are diligent, patient, and diligent in developing new skills that are up to date with the situation, you will be able to overcome the obstacles. However, this year is a year of learning and gaining experience, so you should be determined and observant, ask questions to get information, and take action. Sometimes right, sometimes wrong, all are on the path of learning. Just don't be stubborn and arrogant, people around you will be happy to help. Another equally important thing is not to interfere with the work that is under the responsibility of others. You must also be careful with your words. Everything must be done mindfully and calmly, which will help solve problems. However, during the 3rd Chinese month (April 4 – May 4), the 7th Chinese month (August 7 – September 6), the 8th Chinese month(September 7 – October 7), and the 9th Chinese month (October 8 – November 6), do not be hasty in your assigned work, as mistakes may occur. Whether signing contracts related to studying or work, you should check carefully so that there will be no problems later. In addition, during this period, you should not make new or additional investments. There will be damage for the months when both work and education have a good direction of progress including the 12th Chinese month (January 5 - February 2), the 2nd Chinese month (March 5 - April 3), the 5th Chinese month (June 5 - July 5), and the 6th Chinese month (July 6 - August 6). For seniors, you can find heirs or assistants to help take care of various investments. It will bring good results.

Financial

This year, the financial horoscope of both horoscopes is quite volatile. Therefore, you should spend thriftily for safety. Manage your cash flow to be liquid so that you do not encounter crises. Especially during the months when your finances will be low and sluggish and unexpected expenses will occur, which are the 3rd Chinese month (April 4 - May 4), the 7th Chinese month (August 7 - September 6), the 8th Chinese month (September 7 - October 7), and the 9th Chinese month (October 8 - November 6). Do not lend money or sign a guarantee. Do not gamble or take risks. Do not invest in illegal businesses or businesses related to copyright infringement. This year is especially sensitive and may encounter lawsuits. Therefore, it is best not to get involved. The months when your finances will return to flowing smoothly and you will receive unexpected windfalls are the 12th Chinese month (January 5 – February 2), the 2nd Chinese month (March 5 – April 3), the 5th Chinese month (June 5 – July 5), and the 6th Chinese month (July 6 – August 6).

Family

This year's family horoscope is a bad sign. You should be careful about the health problems of family members and unexpected events that will cause peace in the house. This is because this year, two bad stars will visit you: the Humti star (the star of love) and the Kuahu star (the star of lawsuits). Therefore, you should be careful about accidents and conflicts that lead to lawsuits, all of which will cause distress and discomfort to family members.

In particular, the months when your family will experience chaos are the 3rd Chinese month

(April 4 - May 4), the 7th Chinese month (August 7 - September 6), the 8th Chinese month (September 7 - October 7), and the 9th Chinese month (October 8 - November 6), when the person must be especially patient. If there is a quarrel or dispute, you should try to control your emotions and prevent accidents that may cause injury or bleeding to family members. You should also be careful of subordinates or servants who cause trouble or steal or damage valuables.

In addition, you should keep away from friends who are not in the right and you should not get involved in conflicts between friends. Be careful about going out in groups to hang out in shady places because you may fall victim to a misfortune that you did not cause but end up with a lawsuit. Also, when making friends, you should be careful of friends who do not wish you well and come to deceive you.

Love
For the elders this year, if you act like a banyan tree, not being fussy or intrusive, your children

and grandchildren will respect and love you well. For the young people, this year you are quite charming and will receive attention from many people of the opposite sex. However, at this age, there is still a lot of time to think carefully and consider. It is better than making a hasty decision making a mistake and being disappointed later. Although love is a matter of fate if you have made merit together in the past, no matter what, you will be soulmates. If not, you will have to be separated, so do not think too much. The months when the love of the person with a horoscope is quite fragile and arguments can easily occur are the 3rd Chinese month (April 4 - May 4), the 7th Chinese month (August 7 - September 6), the 8th Chinese month (September 7 - October 7), and the 9th Chinese month (October 8 - November 6), when you should not interfere in other people's family matters. You must also be careful of a third party who may come between you and your lover and cause misunderstandings. In addition, going to entertainment venues You must know how to protect yourself.

Health

This year, health is not good for both seniors and young adults because there will be hidden illnesses. Even if you see a doctor and take medicine, the symptoms will usually improve temporarily. Before long, they will come back again, causing you to have to go in and out of the hospital frequently. Therefore, you should take care of yourself to have immunity against illnesses, get enough sleep, eat healthy food, and find time to exercise appropriately for your age. This year, illnesses you should be careful of are allergies, migraines, and hepatitis. In particular, the months when you need to take special care of your health are the 3rd Chinese month (April 4 – May 4), the 7th Chinese month (August 7 – September 6), the 8th Chinese month (September 7 – October 7), and the 9th Chinese month (October 8 – November 6). Be more attentive to yourself and be careful of accidents both while working and traveling near and far.

Year of the DOG (Fire) | (1958) & (2018)

"The DOG is on the Moutain." is a person born in the year of the DOG at the age of 67 years (1958) and 7 years (2018)

Overview

For seniors, this year all activities that will proceed will not be smooth. Therefore, if you will do anything, you should think carefully and plan carefully. Beware of unexpected accidents that will cause injuries and loss of property. This is the time for you to prepare to step down and hand over your work to your children to take care of instead. You should be careful about health problems, especially pain in the waist and legs. You should also be careful of dizziness and fainting that will cause injury. In terms of work and business, this year there will be obstacles and pressure. For family events, you still need to pay close attention to safety. Traveling, no matter how far or near, please do not be careless. Also, when speaking or teaching your children, you must know how to choose your words because you may unintentionally offend them. It may cause the person being criticized to be hurt and become distant from each other. It is best not to get involved in other people's conflicts or interfere in your children's affairs so that you will be happy and comfortable.

For children of this age, for their studies, you should be attentive and focused. Do not be too selfish. There may be some problems in understanding the lessons, but it is not beyond your ability. Just be attentive and review the lessons often. Be careful of accidents while playing sports, going on field trips, and traveling. You will also need to be careful of accidents that will result in injuries. Also, be careful of the possibility of a fight arising from an argument, so be careful and be safe.

Career and Business

For senior horoscopes, this year, even though there will be obstacles in your work, there will be some opportunities to make a living. However, during the year, you should prepare to find new generations to take over your work because when new generations come to help, there will be creativity and adjustments to create new things and help your work progress smoothly and better, especially during the months when your work will be outstanding and have a good direction of progress, namely the 12th Chinese month (January 5 - February 2), the 2nd Chinese month (March 5 - April 3), the 5th Chinese month (June 5 - July 5), and the 6th Chinese month (July 6 - August 6).

For young children, this year there will be bad stars staring at their zodiac houses. Therefore, even though their studies will progress, parents should talk to their teachers to be informed of their development and any problems that may arise, especially during the months when Both work and study will be hindered and encounter obstacles in the 3rd Chinese month (April 4 – May 4), the 7th Chinese month (August 7 – September 6), the 8th Chinese month (September 7 – October 7), and the 9th Chinese month (October 8 – November 6). During this period, seniors should be careful about making contracts and should delay investing. Beware of dishonest partners in accounting. As for young children during this period, parents should closely supervise them. Be careful not to let them be led astray by ill-wishers or invited by friends to play far away. Parents and guardians must pay special attention.

Financial

This year, due to the planetary disasters, liquidity is quite tight. Income and expenses are volatile and uncertain. There is also a chance of losing money and capital outflow. Some people, like to solve the problem by buying expensive items that they like from the beginning of the year to reduce the power of losing money. Also, be careful during the following months when your finances will be stuck and unexpected expenses will occur, which are the 3rd Chinese month (April 4 - May 4), the 7th Chinese month (August 7 - September 6), the 8th Chinese month (September 7 - October 7), and the 9th Chinese month (October 8 - November 6). Also, this year, you should not be greedy for wealth that is not yours. Gambling, taking risks, or investing in illegal businesses should be avoided. Otherwise, this year, you will be punished and have a lawsuit. In addition, you should be careful not to spend more than you can afford or use future money thinking that you will be able to pay it back in time because this will cause you more problems. Be careful not to be tricked into losing your money when investing. The months when your finances will return to flowing smoothly and you will receive unexpected windfalls are the 12th Chinese month (January 5 – February 2), the 2nd Chinese month (March 5 – April 3), the 5th Chinese month (June 5 – July 5), and the 6th Chinese month (July 6 – August 6).

Family

Since the inauspicious constellations are looking at the family horoscope of the person, the unexpected can happen, such as conflicts, lawsuits, being harmed, or accidents that cause bloodshed, illnesses of family members, and dangers from thieves. In particular, the months when you should be extra careful are the 3rd Chinese month (April 4 – May 4), the 7th Chinese month (August 7 – September 6), the

8th Chinese month (September 7 – October 7), and the 9th Chinese month (October 8 – November 6). In addition, you should be careful about safety in your home, such as damaged fixtures that may fall on you, electrical appliances, and cooking gas that may cause accidents. You should also be careful of subordinates or subordinates who slander you or secretly harm you, causing you injury. You should not get involved in disputes between friends, especially regarding lawsuits.

Love

For seniors and your partner, this year the overall picture is smooth, there are no problems to worry about. But there is an important thing for you, which is your expression and conversation with family members. Do not show emotion and power, but should use kindness as the main principle. Taking care of children sometimes requires love and understanding before using orders to be effective. In some cases, you have to let your children face real events so that they can gain experience. Reprimanding and admonishing young people by complaining that even though you may be right in some things, you may not be right in everything. Therefore, if you can let go, it will be beneficial to you. Your children will respect and love you. Entering the 3rd Chinese month (April 4 - May 4), 7th Chinese month (August 7 - September 6), 8th Chinese month (September 7 - October 7), and 9th Chinese month (October 8 - November 6), do not interfere in other people's family matters. And must be careful of arguing between you and your partner. The time that has passed, living together, right or wrong, has been through both happiness and suffering together. In any case, it is better to be considerate of each other's feelings.

Health
This year, your health is not very good. You should exercise regularly according to your age, get enough rest, and eat nutritious and easily digestible food. Because your horoscope has many inauspicious stars in your zodiac, it will cause more health problems. Be careful of back pain, waist pain, and knee pain. Especially

in the following months, you must pay special attention to your health and that of small children: the 3rd Chinese month (April 4 - May 4), the 7th Chinese month (August 7 - September 6), the 8th Chinese month (September 7 - October 7), and the 9th Chinese month (October 8 - November 6). For the elderly, be careful of heart disease, diabetes, and other hidden diseases. As for small children, when doing activities at home or while traveling outside the home, be careful of unexpected accidents that may cause injuries.

Year of the DOG (Gold) | (1970)
" The Dogs in Morality" is a person born in the year of the DOG at the age of 55 years (1970)

Overview
For the dog horoscope in this age group, this year is considered a year in which you will have outstanding achievements. Your career and business will progress. Therefore, you should not let time pass by in vain. If you consider the appropriate month and are ready in various

aspects, you should seize this opportunity to create achievements, expand branches, increase sales and income, or push forward any projects that you have previously planned. There will be good directions and results in return.

However, during the year, your horoscope house is surrounded by a group of evil stars that will affect your safety, unexpected unusual events, losses, and property losses. You must be more careful when investing in business. There is a chance that you will fall victim to fraudsters who will entice you to invest and cause damage.

You should be more careful within your family about your safety. Check the equipment that is installed and fixed to make sure it is not damaged. If you find that it is not strong, you should immediately replace it or repair it. Do not let it fall and harm people in the house.

Be careful that your subordinates or subordinates will bring you trouble or cause quarrels. Also, you should not use your emotions when contacting people around you. You will unknowingly offend others and cause problems in your work. In addition, you should avoid alcohol and all vices because they can cause problems at work and loss of money. In particular, you should refrain from going to entertainment venues because problems will follow.

Career and Business

Although this year your career and business direction will flourish and progress, there are still pitfalls and hidden traps on the smooth road. Therefore, you must be careful before doing any activities. Take care of internal matters and constantly develop new skills to keep up with the surrounding situations that often change and are beyond your expectations. Study and gain expertise in what you will be responsible for. Place people who are suitable for the job. This will help reduce problems that may occur a lot because there are still other factors that are beyond your control waiting to challenge you. The most important thing that you should not neglect is strengthening relationships with those you have to contact regularly. This will help facilitate many things to go smoothly, reduce damage and reduce conflicts, especially during the 3rd Chinese Month (April 4 - May 4), the 7th Chinese Month (August 7 - September 6), the 8th Chinese Month (September 7 - October 7), and the 9th Chinese Month (October 8 - November 6). Be more careful when investing. Do not be selfish and calculate the possible losses. Also, when making employment contracts or contracts, carefully consider the details. For starting a new job, entering into joint ventures, and investing in various areas. This is an appropriate time to find heirs to continue your career, especially in terms of investment, because combining new and old ideas will help produce positive feedback, especially in the following months when your career and business will see progress: the 12th Chinese month (January 5 - February 2), the 2nd Chinese month (March 5 - April 3), the 5th Chinese month (June 5 - July 5), and the 6th Chinese month (July 6 - August 6).

Financial

This year, the fortune of the person with a financial fortune is in good condition. The cash flow will come in two ways: directly from salary or sales of goods or services, and extra money from special jobs such as commissions, agents, and others. You may also receive money from a windfall. Therefore, you should be diligent and determined to earn money. In particular, the following months when the owner's finances will flow smoothly are the 12th Chinese month (January 5 – February 2), the 2nd Chinese month (March 5 – April 3), the 5th Chinese month (June 5 – July 5), and the 6th Chinese month (July 6 – August 6). However, one should be careful during the months when finances will become sluggish and should plan well to cope with them, namely the 3rd Chinese month (April 4 – May 4), the 7th Chinese month (August 7 – September 6), the 8th Chinese month (September 7 – October 7), and the 9th Chinese month (October 8 – November 6). Do not lend money to others or sign as a financial guarantee. Do not gamble or take risks. Do not invest in illegal businesses because there is a chance of making a mistake and going to jail. In addition, one should be careful of additional damage from investments.

Family
This year, your family will lack peace because of the disturbing energy from the evil stars. Therefore, you should be more careful of unexpected events, accidents, the safety of your family members, and disputes with family members that may lead to lawsuits. In particular, during the months when your family is likely to encounter problems and chaos, namely the 3rd Chinese month (April 4 – May 4), the 7th Chinese month (August 7 – September 6), the 8th Chinese month (September 7 – October 7), and the 9th Chinese month (October 8 – November 6). During these times, you should be more careful in everything, including problems of illness in your family. You should also find ways to prevent accidents that may occur. Be careful of losing valuables, being stolen, or falling victim to scammers. Be careful of subordinates or servants causing trouble. Also, do not get

involved in conflicts between friends, especially in matters related to lawsuits.

Love

This year, the basic love horoscope is not very good due to the influence of inauspicious stars that often send negative energy to make your married life chaotic. Your mind tends to seek vices, alcohol, and being charmed by the opposite sex who is not your partner. Especially during the months when your love is quite fragile and arguments are easily caused, namely the 3rd Chinese month (April 4 – May 4), the 7th Chinese month (August 7 – September 6), the 8th Chinese month (September 7 – October 7), and the 9th Chinese month (October 8 – November 6). During these months, you should be careful about arguments. You should not get involved in other people's husbands and wives. Do not be gullible and listen to gossip or slander your lover. It is better to face each other and talk to each other with reason. Do not use emotions and should not lie because it will make the matter worse. In addition, during these months, if the person goes to seek entertainment at entertainment venues, they should know how to protect themselves. Be careful not to get infected and get sick.

Health

This year, the health of this person is not very good. They tend to get sick often. Be careful of old and new diseases, such as back pain, pain in the waist, and tumors. You should observe for abnormalities in your body. If you find anything unusual, you should see a doctor for diagnosis and treatment. This will help cure the disease quickly. However, you should not be careless with your life. You should take good care of your diet and lifestyle. Be careful of infectious diseases that may enter your mouth or from eating too much for a long time and accumulating diseases. The months when your health will show symptoms are the 3rd Chinese month (April 4 - May 4), the 7th Chinese month (August 7 - September 6), the 8th Chinese month (September 7 - October 7), and the 9th Chinese month (October 8 - November 6). Observe for abnormalities in your body while working and traveling outside, both near and far. You should also be careful of unexpected accidents.

Year of the DOG (Gold) | (1982)

" The Dog loves the home. " is a person born in the year of the DOG at the age of 43 years (1982)

Overview

This year, the direction of your career and business is good. There is an opportunity to expand your work, expand your business, or show your work for people around you to admire. Overall, this is still a good opportunity to pioneer and start something new because you will receive support from your patrons. However, you must be careful with your words that will affect others and cause problems to come back to you. You must also be careful of friends who are fickle and will bring disaster to you. In addition, work that involves illegal items, tax evasion, or copyrighted products should be careful of lawsuits, which is a result of the power of the evil star Guo Hu.

It is best to do business straightforwardly. Paying taxes, and applying for or renewing licenses should be done correctly. You should also avoid getting involved in anything that is considered illegal, including documents and contracts that you must read and check the details carefully to prevent problems later.

For the family, auspicious energy will appear at home. You will receive good news or there may be a chance to organize an auspicious event this year. However, in terms of health, be careful of falling ill from illness. Love is not very smooth. You should refrain from going out and should find more time to take care of each other. Beware of a third party interfering and destroying peace. Also, be careful of accidents when traveling on the road. Drinking alcohol will cause bad consequences. Visiting entertainment venues will cause a chance of contracting a serious disease.

Career and Business

This year's career is a path of progress. For those who work regularly, there will be an opportunity to be promoted. For those who do business, it will be smooth. Business is good and profitable. There is an opportunity to raise the status to another level. Especially during the months when the career of the person's horoscope is outstanding and prosperous, namely, the 12th Chinese month (January 5 - February 2), the 2nd Chinese month (March 5 - April 3), the 5th Chinese month (June 5 - July 5), and the 6th Chinese month (July 6 - August 6). In addition, the aforementioned period is suitable for investing in new businesses, which are expected to yield returns that are worth the investment. However, you should be careful during the following months when your work will have unexpected changes and obstacles, including:

3rd Chinese Month (April 4 – May 4), 7th Chinese Month (August 7 – September 6), the 8th Chinese Month (September 7 – October 7), and 9th Chinese Month (October 8 – November 6).

The important thing this year is that you must use good human relations skills to communicate in your work. Be careful not to use emotions to make decisions about various problems because it will only make the problems worse. When making employment contracts or hiring contracts, you should carefully consider the details of the contract before deciding to sign. In addition, during this period, you should be careful about joint investments that use numerical benefits as an incentive, when in fact, they are just castles in the air. If you get lost in joint investment, you will lose more than gain.

Financial

Although this year has quite a good cash flow, in the middle of the year there will be unexpected large expenses interfering and financial leakages, causing cash flow to lack liquidity. Therefore, at the beginning of the year, if you manage your income and expenses systematically and have a good plan, it will help you not run out of money, especially during the 3rd Chinese month (April 4 - May 4), the 7th

Chinese month (August 7 - September 6), the 8th Chinese month (September 7 - October 7), and the 9th Chinese month (October 8 - November 6), when you should not gamble, do not lend money to people close to you, do not be greedy for profits that do not belong to you, and do not invest in businesses that are suspicious or infringe on copyrights because you may not be able to escape lawsuits. In addition, investing is risky, so you should delay investing. The months when your finances are liquid are the 12th Chinese month (January 5 – February 2), the 2nd Chinese month (March 5 – April 3), the 5th Chinese month (June 5 – July 5), and the 6th Chinese month (July 6 – August 6).

Family

This year, your family's horoscope is good but hiding evil. You should be careful of the safety of your family members and any unexpected events that might occur. Be careful of family members getting injured in accidents. Be careful of arguments that might lead to legal disputes. Be careful that a good relationship with your neighbors that has been going well will reach a turning point. Especially during the months when your family will encounter problems and chaos, namely the 3rd Chinese month (April 4 – May 4), the 7th Chinese month (August 7 – September 6), the 8th Chinese month (September 7 – October 7), and the 9th Chinese month (October 8 – November 6). Be careful of illnesses and diseases of people in the family. Be careful of subordinates causing trouble and be careful of losing valuables or falling victim to scammers. Additionally, you should distance yourself from friends who like to disturb you. Do not get involved in your friends' disputes, especially legal disputes, because it will be difficult to withdraw and it will only make you suffer like bringing lice on your head.

Love

This year, your love life is not smooth. You and your partner will often argue. In addition, using sarcastic words to hurt your partner will create deep hurt in your heart. This is an invisible danger that you should be careful of. In addition, the influence of the stars often makes the person want to go out and wander. Leaving your partner alone at home is a serious enemy to love. Therefore, you should be more considerate and considerate of your partner. Be careful that a third party may come in between and cause problems that make you not want to look at each other. This is especially true in the 3rd Chinese month (April 4 - May 4), the 7th Chinese month (August 7 - September 6), the 8th Chinese month (September 7 - October 7), and the 9th Chinese month (October 8 - November 6), when you will have to put in extra effort to maintain your married life. Think before you speak. Do not interfere in other people's family matters. Be careful of going to entertainment venues because there is a chance of catching a serious disease.

Health

This year, your overall health is quite good. It may be because people with money are comfortable and healthy. However, you should be careful because, during the year, the evil star "Tiang Ae" (the danger star) will appear and move to look at your health base. Therefore, you should be careful of dangers and injuries from unexpected events. In particular, the months when you should pay extra attention to your health are the 3rd Chinese month (April 4 – May 4), the 7th Chinese month (August 7 – September 6), the 8th Chinese month (September 7 – October 7), and the 9th Chinese month (October 8 – November 6). You should be more careful of the dangers of injuries from accidents while traveling and using the road, and from being attacked due to impatience or being hit by a stray bullet.

Year of the DOG (Water) | (1994)
"The dog is guarding the house." is a person born in the year of the DOG at the age of 31 years (1994)

Overview
For the dog year of this age, this year is another year that you must control your body and mind to be mindful. Do not act carelessly or stray. You cannot be hasty in your work or activities because there may be dangers and troubles.

You should be careful with your words and manners that may offend others without realizing it. Even though the impact you receive from the inauspicious star will cause you to lose money and often forget yourself. You may want to go out when invited or have other motivations that will make you careless in your life and may cause accidents. The "Hong Sua Star" will cause unexpected disasters, accidents, and disasters. The "Xiao Ying Star" will affect subordinates or servants who cause problems or there will be ill-wishers who come to disturb and cause various things. But it is considered lucky that in your horoscope, auspicious stars are shining.

These two stars will help and support you in many things, making you mindful and have special powers to increase your work efficiency. You will also find support from adults, so you should be diligent and persevering. You will have the opportunity to be considered for a promotion and a salary increase from your superior or supervisor in the department. There will also be times when you will receive the power to build yourself up. For those who want to have their own business, you should seize this good time, plan, and always improve your skills to keep up with the situation. You must not be impatient or rash. Use your human relations to your advantage. Be diligent and determined to reach your goal because this year has a path of progress. If you are not persistent at this time, you will miss a good opportunity, which is a pity.

Career and Business

This year, the career of the person will find a patron. Therefore, the job will progress. The business will flourish. Therefore, you should be diligent in earning and saving, constantly developing yourself and increasing your knowledge. Know how to catch the right timing and opportunities, especially during the months when the career will progress and flourish, which are the 12th Chinese month (January 5 - February 2), the 2nd Chinese month (March 5 - April 3), the 5th Chinese month (June 5 - July 5), and the 6th Chinese month (July 6 - August 6). Although there are many good times for investing or joining a joint venture, if you study all aspects and follow the situation mindfully and with awareness, it will help reduce risks and reduce the chances of loss. In particular, the months when your work will encounter obstacles and problems are the 3rd Chinese month (April 4 – May 4), the 7th Chinese month (August 7 – September 6), the 8th Chinese month (September 7 – October 7), and the 9th Chinese month (October 8 – November 6) where you will be affected by the evil stars. This group of evil stars will cause a lack of concentration in your work, problems and obstacles will interfere, and conflicts will often occur in your work. You will also find subordinates causing you damage and suffering. If you have to back down from some work, you should back down. If you are stubborn and stubborn, be careful or you will lose your job. If some work requires time, you should not be impatient. You should be more careful in your work activities and not let your emotions lead to reason. When signing any contract, you should consider it carefully. Be careful of hidden details that will put you at a disadvantage. In addition, you should delay investing during this period because there is a chance of being cheated. You will also encounter accounting fraud and harassment from ill-wishers.

Financial

This year, even though it is a good income criterion, it is good with the condition that you have to be diligent in your work to get it. Therefore, under the financial horoscope that promotes you, you should increase your diligence in seeking to make income flow densely. The income will flow in two ways, both directly from salary or sales of products or services and from special work, special income, including money from windfalls, especially during the following months when your finances will flow smoothly, namely, the 12th Chinese month (January 5 - February 2), the 2nd Chinese month (March 5 - April 3), the 5th Chinese month (June 5 - July 5), and the 6th Chinese month (July 6 - August 6). Therefore, you should not be indifferent and miss opportunities. However, you should be careful during the months when your finances will be tight, which are the 3rd Chinese month (April 4 – May 4), the 7th Chinese month (August 7 – September 6), the 8th Chinese month (September 7 – October 7), and the 9th Chinese month (October 8 – November 6). Do not gamble, lend money sign financial guarantees, or invest in illegal businesses. Be careful of a lack of liquidity in your working capital. Also, do not be greedy for illicit gains. Most importantly, you should set aside some money for emergency savings.

Family

This year, your family will lack peace. Beware of health problems of the elderly in the house and unexpected accidents, especially in the following months when there will be chaos and trouble in the family: the 3rd Chinese month (April 4 - May 4), the 7th Chinese month (August 7 - September 6), the 8th Chinese month (September 7 - October 7), and the 9th Chinese month (October 8 - November 6). Find ways to prevent accidents that will affect family members. Maintain good relationships both in the house and with neighbors. Beware of subordinates causing trouble. Also, you should keep your valuables hidden. Beware of people in the house who are quick to snatch things. Also, beware of dangers from criminals. Also, beware of friends with bad intentions who may secretly spread slanderous news or try to harm you.

Love
In terms of love, things are good enough. Be careful of ill-wishers who slander and incite misunderstandings. Therefore, you should be firm and not gullible. You should check the facts and speak with reason. Try not to fight back against the other person. This will help calm down the argument and then try to understand each other again later. In addition, be careful of a third party interfering in your love life, especially during the months when love is weak and fragile, which are the 3rd Chinese month (April 4 – May 4), the 7th Chinese month (August 7 – September 6), the 8th Chinese month (September 7 – October 7), and the 9th Chinese month (October 8 – November 6). The

person must be careful of arguments that may escalate and not get involved in other couples' families. Avoid going to entertainment venues because you may bring back sickness and troubles as a bonus.

Health

This year your overall health is fair, but you should still take care of your eating and drinking hygiene because you may catch an infectious disease or fall ill from an epidemic. Be careful of accidents both while working and traveling, especially during the months when you need to take extra care of your health, which are the 3rd Chinese month (April 4 - May 4), the 7th Chinese month (August 7 - September 6), the 8th Chinese month (September 7 - October 7), and the 9th Chinese month (October 8 - November 6). Be extra careful of unexpected events because you may suffer injuries or bleeding.

Chinese Astrology Horoscope for Each Month

Month 12 in the Dragon Year (5 Jan 25 - 2 Feb 25)

This month, you should have a goal and plan to support both your work and budget. This month is considered another good time that is smooth as if you have received a blessing from the gods. In addition, many auspicious stars will appear in orbit and shine into your horoscope house, resulting in both finance and business smoothness. Obstacles and problems that have been stuck in the past year will find supporters. You will receive cooperation from your elders and colleagues, allowing your work to proceed smoothly. On this occasion, you must prepare a project to expand during the period when your horoscope is rising. Because during this time, the more you do, the more you will receive. If you increase your diligence in creating results or speed up sales, along with diligently increasing your new skills and knowledge to keep up with the situation, you will have a greater chance of seeing good returns. For those born in the Year of the Dog who are thinking of opening a shop or having their own business, you can choose to start this month because it has good supporting power.

In terms of finances, it is smooth. Cash flow will flow in two ways: salary and increased sales, as well as extra money from special jobs and windfall luck. This month, liquidity is high. However, you should always save money, for emergencies, so that you will not be in trouble or financial difficulty. For various investments, This period will bring good returns.

Family, this month there will be an auspicious time to move into a new house. There will be happy news regarding auspicious family events.

Love will blossom and bear fruit. The path will be smooth and bright like a bed of rose petals.

Health will be strong and free from illnesses, but if there are any, they will be easy to treat.

Support Days: 1 Jan., 5 Jan., 9 Jan., 13 Jan., 17 Jan., 21 Jan., 25 Jan., 29 Jan
Lucky Days: 10 Jan., 22 Jan.
Misfortune Days: 11 Jan., 21 Jan.
Bad Days: 2 Jan., 4 Jan., 14 Jan., 16 Jan., 26 Jan., 28 Jan.

Month 1 in the Snake Year (3 Feb 25 - 4 Mar 25)
This month, those born in the year of the dog will experience a mix of good and bad things. Although your career and business will encounter storms and your harvest will be damaged, some things will still be left. What you should be concerned about is the safety and health of your family members. What you should do during this period is to inspect the things installed in your house, such as the roof or other furniture, to see if they are still strong. Also, check electrical appliances and gas stoves to see if they are safe. If anything is damaged, you must quickly buy and replace them or repair them. Don't let the cows run away and then lock the barn door.

In terms of your career and business, during this period, you will have to work harder than usual. However, if you don't do it, you will lose more money. Therefore, if you work harder, you will not only not lose money, but you will also find that you will have profit left.

In terms of finances, this month, income will flow in normally. However, you must maintain diligence and perseverance, find new ways to increase your income and make money grow. You should not be greedy for wealth that is not yours or greedy for only a little bit. You will be persuaded to lose a large sum of money that is not worth it. Starting a new job and investing in stocks are not good.

In terms of your family, during this period, it is important to be careful of health problems and accidents. And will encounter uninvited guests causing trouble. In addition, valuables are likely to be damaged, lost, or stolen.

Love's horoscope is smooth. Your lover will take care of you and be your advisor and help you. Health horoscope must be careful of accidents and dangers from traveling.

Support Days: 2 Feb., 6 Feb., 10 Feb., 14 Feb., 18 Feb., 22 Feb., 26 Feb.
Lucky Days: 3 Feb., 15 Feb., 27 Feb.
Misfortune Days: 4 Feb., 16 Feb., 28 Feb.
Bad Days: 7 Feb., 9 Feb., 19 Feb., 21 Feb.

Month 2 in the Snake Year (5 Mar 25 - 3 Apr 25)
This month, your horoscope trend may have improved, but your career and business will still have problems that keep you from making up your mind. Many problems and obstacles have not been resolved. What you should do during this period is to consult with experts and experience or ask for help from business partners. At the very least, there will be a way out and help to solve and ease the problem from serious to light.

In terms of work, it is like sitting in the dawn near the sunrise, which is a good sign of a new day. Therefore, this period is like warming up, waiting for the right moment and opportunity. Prepare all your resources to be ready, increase your skills and knowledge in areas that you lack, and take good care of your work and responsibilities. When the month that supports you arrives, you can invest or operate at full power. You will be successful.

Your income this month will be better but don't expect too much from gambling and taking risks on unexpected windfalls. In any case, you should adhere to the principle of sufficiency and be frugal. Any unnecessary expenses should be cut off. In addition, you should closely manage and take care of your capital liquidity. Starting a new job, investing in shares, or investing in various areas, this period will find a way to make money.

Peaceful family horoscope If there are obstacles, you will find a patron to help.

Health-wise, you will encounter problems with gastritis, intestinal diseases, and food poisoning. Therefore, do not drink or eat excessively and should take good care of hygiene.

In terms of love, the time of charm has come again. During this time, you will have many opportunities to be close and have relationships with the opposite sex. Use your "mind" before your "heart" when considering who to associate with. Worried today will be relieved tomorrow. Also, do not interfere in other people's married lives.

Support Days: Mar, 6 Mar., 10 Mar., 14 Mar., 18 Mar., 22 Mar., 26 Mar., 30 Mar.
Lucky Days: 11 Mar, 23 Mar.
Misfortune Days: 12 Mar, 24 Mar.
Bad Days: 3 Mar, 5 Mar., 15 Mar., 17 Mar., 27 Mar., 29 Mar.

Month 3 in the Snake Year (4 Apr 25 - 4 May 25)
This month, your horoscope will encounter conflicts. Although there will be obstacles and problems, overall, all work activities will still have a path of progress because you will find a

patron. On this occasion, what you should do is quickly solve problems and complete pending work. In addition, you should build friendships and relationships with business partners, customers, and business associates. Find a way to form a business alliance to help and rely on each other during the crisis.

In terms of work, you will encounter both small and chaotic obstacles and personal conflicts. When signing various contracts, be careful not to be deceived or tricked into falling victim to fraud. Starting a new job, entering into joint ventures, and investing in various projects this month will have a bad direction.

In terms of finances, this month you will be in a position to lose money. The person with this horoscope may resolve the bad omen by paying for expensive things that they like from the beginning of the month to resolve the bad omen of losing money. In addition, you should not gamble take risks, or expect unexpected gains this month. Also, do not lend money to others or be a guarantor for anyone because there is a chance of getting hurt. In addition, you should spend money carefully and not be greedy. When you have money, you should also think about when you are in need. If possible, you should set aside some money to make merit. This will help many things go smoothly.

In terms of family, there is a lack of peace. Beware of disputes that may arise and become lawsuits, requiring you to go to court to resolve the case. You should inspect and take care of the safety of your home and be more careful of accidents.

In terms of love, you will find a third party interfering, causing arguments. You should not go to entertainment venues.

In terms of health, you will easily get sick. Beware of allergies, infectious diseases, and accumulated diseases from neglecting to take care of yourself for a long time. Also, be careful of accidents when traveling.

Support Days: 3 Apr., 7 Apr., 11 Apr., 15 Apr., 19 Apr., 23 Apr., 27 Apr.
Lucky Days: 4 Apr., 16 Apr., 28 Apr.
Misfortune Days: 5 Apr., 17 Apr., 29 Apr.
Bad Days: 8 Apr., 10 Apr., 20 Apr., 22 Apr.

Month 4 in the Snake Year (5 May 25 - 4 Jun 25)
This month, obstacles in your work will become more apparent, causing problems in other activities to increase, which will affect your cash flow. What you should do now is to save money in every activity to maintain the liquidity that is still in the system. Always remember that to get through the crisis and problems, you must be mindful, prioritize problems, and make decisions decisively. Do not use emotions. For work or business, this month is a time to be diligent to make up for the work that was reduced from the previous month. You should also visit customers, business partners, and those you need to contact to strengthen your relationship.

Although your finances this month are moderate, you should still not use your money to gamble on various matters. Also, do not be kind enough to lend money to anyone and help guarantee for you.

You should also not invest in businesses that violate the law or are related to copyright. Most importantly, you should manage your assets well and set aside some money for emergency savings. As for working together or investing, this month there will be new interesting opportunities, but you should seek advice from knowledgeable and experienced people before making a decision.

Overall, your family is going smoothly, but this month you must be careful of problems from servants or servants in the house that will cause problems and bring trouble.

For love, is in the period of blossoming and fruitfulness. The love tree is growing brightly. This is a good opportunity for singles to develop their relationship. However, for those who have a partner, you must be mindful and firm. Do not be carried away by the stimuli that come your way.

Your health is in good condition. Even though you may get sick, you will recover in no time.

Support Days: 1 May, 5 May, 9 May, 13 May, 17 May, 21 May, 25 May, 29 May
Lucky Days: 10 May, 22 May
Misfortune Days: 11 May, 23 May
Bad Days: 2 May, 4 May, 14 May, 16 May, 26 May, 28 May

Month 5 in the Snake Year (5 Jun 25 - 6 Jul 25)

This month, your life path has an auspicious star orbiting to shine, which helps many things that have been stuck to improve. Therefore, during this period, you should increase your diligence, and develop yourself in various skills and knowledge that you do not dare to do yet. You have to start doing it. Use this opportunity to your advantage. Try to walk in a new business path or expand and branch out from the current one, which is a good trend. And if you want to make it even better, you should listen to other people's opinions to collect information that will be useful for your future work. In terms of collaboration or investment, this period will have good returns. Starting a new job, joining a joint venture, and investing in various things is a good time.

For financial luck, this month is quite good. The cash flow will flow in two ways, both from your regular salary and sales. There is also a chance to receive extra money from luck. You can invest heavily, but you should not be careless or greedy.

Your family's horoscope is bright with the power of patronage. There will be an opportunity to buy expensive property or there may be a little member in the house. You have a chance to move into a new house, it may be a new house or workplace, or there will be an auspicious event. You will receive good news from family members. Regarding relatives and friends, things are good. If there are any obstacles, you will receive cooperation and help. There is also an opportunity to travel or join merit-making ceremonies.

Health is good enough, but don't be careless. Exercise regularly and eat healthy food.

For love, this is a good time to take your partner on a vacation. For singles, this is a good time to ask for love. If you have made up your mind, don't let the other person wait too long. Be careful of someone who might grab you. But for those who are dating, this month is a good opportunity to get engaged and get married.

Support Days: 2 Jun., 6 Jun., 10 Jun., 14 Jun., 18 Jun., 22 Jun., 26 Jun., 30 Jun.
Lucky Days: 3 Jun., 15 Jun., 27 Jun.
Misfortune Days: 4 Jun., 16 Jun., 28 Jun..
Bad Days: 7 Jun., 9 Jun., 19 Jun., 21 Jun.

Month 6 in the Snake Year (7 Jul 25 - 6 Aug 25)
Entering this month, which is a friendly month for the person of the horoscope, there is an auspicious star orbiting the zodiac sign of the

month, causing pressures and problems to be solved by someone. Projects that you have planned before will be able to be picked up and pushed forward again. What you should do during this period is to increase your diligence, create work, increase sales, and increase your income. This is a challenging period and you can fully demonstrate your abilities. Strike while the iron is hot. When the opportunity comes, if you let it slip away, it will be a pity because your work during this period is receiving support and encouragement.

As for the fortune and financial luck of the person in the horoscope this month, it is quite good and colorful. Whether it is speculation or gambling, there is still a chance. But since it is not a big fortune, please do not be too greedy. As for starting a new job, joining a joint venture, or investing, this period can be done. The expected profits will be as desired.

Within the family, there is peace and mutual support. In addition, you are likely to receive good news about the success of family members. And during this period, it is another month that you have an auspicious time to move into a new house or workplace, redecorate the house, or repair some damaged areas to be in good condition. For some families, there may be criteria for organizing auspicious events for family members during this period. Regarding relatives, this month is good. There will be an opportunity to work together to create new businesses. Otherwise, you will receive useful advice to promote your career and business to progress.

In terms of love and relationships, sweetness will return. Therefore, please cherish this time. Forgive each other for the slightest troubles so that there will only be happy smiles and laughter.

Support Days: 4 Jul., 8 Jul., 12 Jul., 16 Jul., 20 Jul., 24 Jul., 28 Jul.
Lucky Days: 9 Jul., 21 Jul.
Misfortune Days: 10 Jul., 22 Jul.
Bad Days: 1 Jul., 3 Jul., 13 Jul., 15 Jul., 25 Jul., 27 Jul.

Month 7 in the Snake Year (7 Aug 25 - 6 Sep 25)
This month, your life graph is plummeting like you are running out of energy. Many activities that you should push forward are difficult to predict. There are also many bad stars orbiting in your horoscope house, which will cause many things to be uncertain. Career and business, be careful of unexpected changes. Also, be careful of lawsuits, disputes, and accidents. What you should do now is to look at every activity clearly before stepping forward. Be mindful, adjust yourself, and try to find a way to prevent and deal with various situations with caution. Some things take time to handle, so you should be patient and wait. You cannot be impatient. You should also take good care of your work and not interfere with others' work. In terms of accepting or giving orders, you should communicate clearly so that mistakes and damages do not happen. You should also not overlook small points in contracts that may cause problems in the future.

In terms of finance, direct income is normal. Gambling is high-risk. You should manage your working capital well, and allocate some for savings, some for investment, and some for spending appropriately. Also, do not gamble, and do not be greedy for profits that are not yours. As for starting a new job, joining a joint venture, and investing, this month is not suitable. You should postpone it.

Although your family horoscope this month is peaceful, don't be careless with the underlings who like to snatch things.

In terms of health, you have to be careful of accidents on the road. This month, you should not go out to socialize with friends because you might get caught in the crossfire and have bad luck or get dragged into a lawsuit unintentionally.

Support Days: 1 Aug., 5 Aug., 9 Aug., 13 Aug., 17 Aug., 21 Aug., 25 Aug., 29 Aug.
Lucky Days: 2 Aug., 14 Aug., 26 Aug
Misfortune Days: 3 Aug., 15 Aug., 27 Aug
Bad Days: 6 Aug., 8 Aug., 18 Aug, 20 Aug., 30 Aug.

Month 8 in the Snake Year (7 Sep 25 - 7 Oct 25)

This month, your horoscope may look good on the outside, but it is good that hides evil because there is a group of evil stars orbiting in the zodiac house. However, you are lucky to have auspicious stars shining to help. What you should pay attention to this month is to remind yourself to be calm and solve problems immediately. You should be careful and control yourself, especially in matters that will cause you to argue with your partner. You should avoid them. Put yourself in their shoes. Think about the days you shared happiness and sorrow. You should not get involved in other people's family problems. Do not go to entertainment venues. In addition, you will lose money. During this time, there is a chance of getting sick and causing trouble.

In terms of work, you will encounter storms. There will be conflicts and unrest at work. Be careful that your words do not affect others and cause obstacles in your work. In terms of finances this month, even though you will find a patron, you should stand on your own two feet. It will be safer. You will have difficulties today, but in the long run, you will be strong and stable.

In terms of finances, this month is not good. You earn a little and spend a lot. Therefore, you should save money and check for financial leaks so that you do not have to face more financial problems. You should also not lend money to others or sign as a guarantor for anyone. Gambling and taking risks are prohibited. Do not get involved in pirated products or illegal businesses because there will be legal threats. Investments are not good. Investments are not good.

For family matters, be careful of arguments in the house or people in the house fighting with neighbors. Be careful of subordinates or servants causing trouble. Be careful of valuables being damaged, lost, or falling victim to scammers. Relatives, be careful of words that may cause disagreements.

Health-wise, there will be minor illnesses. You still need to be strict about taking care of yourself and refraining from indulging your desires.

Support Days: 2 Sep, 6 Sep., 10 Sep, 14 Sep, 18 Sep., 22 Sep., 26 Sep., 30 Sep.
Lucky Days: 7 Sep, 19 Sep.
Misfortune Days: 8 Sep, 20 Sep.
Bad Days: 1 Sep, 11 Sep., 13 Sep, 23 Sep., 25 Sep.

Month 9 in the Snake Year (8 Oct 25 - 6 Nov 25)
The path of life of the person entering this month has encountered conflicting powers. In addition, there is an appearance of the evil star Guo Hu (the star of lawsuits) that is orbiting to focus and harass, causing the horoscope to fall from its normal line. Therefore, during this period, you should be careful of accidents, lawsuits with criminal penalties, conflicts and arguments, and obstacles in your work.
Negotiations and business contacts often have problems that hinder you. At this time, what

you should do is stay calm and manage your work to survive. It would not be good to help others but cause your work to be ruined. Also, do not show off too much. Many activities during this period require patience and endurance to overcome the crisis.

In terms of finances, during this period, there will be a slump in money, so you should spend thriftily, cut unnecessary and extravagant expenses, and closely monitor your financial statements. This is also another month when you should not lend money to others, not sign as a guarantor or gamble, and not do illegal business because you may not be able to escape imprisonment.

In terms of work, this month, you will encounter obstacles because the star of quarrels enters your horoscope. Therefore, you should be careful of conflicts that may escalate to quarrels.

Therefore, those who do business, especially those who have to contact customers or other people frequently, must be especially careful with their words. In addition, be careful of being investigated by government agencies. You should do everything according to the law. Be careful of subordinates or servants causing trouble.

As for love, there will be arguments. Think back to when you first fell in love and talk things out.

For those who have a family, during this time you must be patient, avoid arguing, and avoid going out to entertainment venues at night.

In terms of health, be careful of stomach diseases, heart disease, and accidents both while working and traveling.

In terms of relatives, starting a new job, joint ventures, and various investments are still not in a good direction.

Support Days: 4 Oct., 8 Oct., 12 Oct., 16 Oct., 20 Oct., 24 Oct., 28 Oct.
Lucky Days: 1 Oct., 13 Oct., 25 Oct.

Misfortune Days: 2 Oct., 14 Oct., 26 Oct.
Bad Days: 5 Oct., 7 Oct., 17 Oct., 19 Oct., 29 Oct., 31 Oct.

Month 10 in the Snake Year (7 Nov 25 - 6 Dec 25)

This month, bad stars are gathering and staring at your zodiac sign. Your fate will fluctuate up and down, lacking certainty. What you should do on this occasion is to not act hastily or impulsively in your work or activities during this period, and to do it within your abilities and resources. Do not interfere with the work of others to reduce the obstacles or hindrances that may arise.

Even though your career is not progressing during this period, and your business is still stable, you should maintain your current position and not be left behind. You must also supervise and communicate your work with your subordinates or subordinates in your department well so that your work will not be damaged or mistakes will occur. You should also be careful when signing contracts so that you will not be at a disadvantage. In addition, you should observe the popularity of your products and consumer needs, study the market, and analyze your competitors clearly so that you can make timely changes so that you will not lag behind others.

Your salary horoscope is still not good. Do not lend money to anyone or be a guarantor for someone close to you. You have the right to be responsible for them. As for joint ventures or investments, you should avoid them during this period because you have the right to get hurt.

But for the family horoscope, during this period, you are lucky to find auspicious stars to help you, resulting in your hopes and dreams going smoothly.

In terms of health, you are quite weak, your resistance is reduced, and you will easily get sick. If you get sick, please do not leave it for too long because if it gets worse, it will be even harder to treat.

For love, do not be cold and indifferent. Expect the other person to do something. You should start by being a giver first. Do not test your jealousy with your partner, it will only cause arguments in the long run. Also, avoid going to entertainment venues.

Support Days: 1 Nov., 5 Nov., 9 Nov., 13 Nov., 17 Nov., 21 Nov., 25 Nov., 29 Nov.
Lucky Days: 6 Nov., 18 Nov., 30 Nov.
Misfortune Days: 7 Nov., 19 Nov.
Bad Days: 10 Nov., 12 Nov., 22 Nov., 24 Nov.

Month 11 in the Snake Year (7 Dec 25 - 4 Jan 26)
This month, your horoscope is in a shaky phase. Things that you expected to happen may change and be unstable. All activities during this period should be considered carefully and thought carefully before doing anything. In terms of your career and business, there will be ups and downs. You should use your strengths rather than relying on others for help. What you should do during this period is that those who do business or trade should closely

monitor situations that are beyond their control and changes in the market. Study information to know it thoroughly so that you do not make mistakes or cause damage. Especially in terms of stock, because even though you sold a lot last month, your horoscope is still fluctuating up and down, causing sales to be inconsistent. This will cause a lot of stock to remain in stock. In addition to causing money to be stuck, it will also cause a liquidity problem.

This month, your financial horoscope is moderate. There will be a small amount of unexpected money, but if you are greedy, the money may disappear. There will be a period of liquidity shortage. Therefore, you should not lend money to others or be a guarantor for anyone.

In terms of work, even though you will encounter obstacles, you must persist in pushing your work forward without letting it stumble. You should also be careful of conflicts between people at work. If you encounter problems, you must immediately resolve them decisively. Do not leave them untreated because they will become chronic problems that are difficult to cure. This month is not suitable for investment.

For a peaceful family, health-wise, beware of latent illnesses and overwork that may cause you to fall ill. Also, do not be careless with accidents while working and traveling. Regarding relatives and friends, beware of new friends who may disturb you without any consideration. Also, beware of those who wish you harm or stab you in the back.

In terms of love, there will be conflicts during this period. You should be firm and not be easily influenced. Do not get carried away by temporary happiness and favors that may cause you to be distracted. Do not get involved with other people's spouses. Avoid going to entertainment venues because you may catch an illness.

Support Days: 3 Dec., 7 Dec., 11 Dec., 15 Dec., 19 Dec., 23 Dec., 27 Dec., 31 Dec.
Lucky Days: 12 Dec., 24 Dec.
Misfortune Days: 1 Dec., 13 Dec., 25 Dec.
Bad Days: 4 Dec., 6 Dec., 16 Dec., 18 Dec., 28 Dec., 30 Dec.

Amulet for The Year of the Dog
"Lord Ganesha is successful in all things."

Those born in the year of the dog this year should set up and worship the sacred object "Lord Ganesha, Success in All Things" to enhance their destiny. Place it on your work desk or cash desk to ask for his power and authority to protect you from dangers, and eliminate bad things, and all dangers that will affect you this year. Ask for his blessing to grant you wealth, fortune, and peace.

In a chapter on advanced Feng Shui, it is mentioned that the deity who will come down to reside in the Mie Keng (House of Destiny) of the year is a deity who can bring both good and bad things to you. Therefore, worshiping to enhance your destiny with a deity who comes down to reside in your birth year is considered to have the best results and the most impact on you. This is to rely on the power of that deity to help protect you while your destiny is declining and having bad luck to alleviate it. At the same time, ask for his blessing to help your business and trade run smoothly as desired, and bring glory and prosperity to you and your family.

For those born in the year of the dog or Mie Keng (horoscope house) in the Suk zodiac, this year is considered an excellent year for you to start a new career or do a side job. Your financial luck is also good. What you need to be careful about is exploding with emotions at others, which will cause a small matter to become a long one. However, since many inauspicious stars are harassing you, this will cause you to lose money and assets. Starting a new job or investing this year, you need to add new skills that are up to date with the situation. Think carefully because there is a high chance of loss. The "Hong Sua Star" will cause you disaster. Be careful of your daily safety and that of your family members. When using the road, be careful of accidents. Avoid causing problems that challenge others, which will bring disaster to yourself. The "Xiao Ying Star" will cause ill-wishers to cause problems and various issues. Your work will be affected and there will be obstacles. Fortunately, in your horoscope, the auspicious star "Thian Koi" will support and help you, which will help ease the burden. However, when making friends with close relatives and friends this year, you still need to analyze and consider people carefully because you may be tricked and harmed. In all activities, you cannot set your hopes too high because there is a chance of fluctuations. In terms of love, it is rather dull and distant. You and your lover will have more frequent disagreements. In terms of health, be careful of accidents while stepping down the stairs. If you want to solve or alleviate disasters, you should set up and worship "Lord Ganesha, Success in All Matters" to ask for his power and authority to help eliminate all bad luck bring peace, and wealth, and increase power and fortune to the person of destiny.

The Tibetan god of fortune is called "Jambala" or as Thais know him "Setthi Shambhala". In Tibet, five "Jambala" gods bestow fortune, happiness, and wealth on humans. Each god has a different appearance: Black Chai Xing,

Red Chai Xing, Green Chai Xing, Yellow Chai Xing, and White Chai Xing.

"Red God Cai Xing" is one of the Hindu gods of fortune, or "Lord Ganesha". According to the beliefs of the Tantric sect, "Red God Cai Xing" is considered the god of the precepts in Tibet and is considered another part of "Vajra Bodhisattva". His appearance has the head of an elephant, two arms, and holds a mongoose in his left hand. Some appearances have three faces, four or six arms, and four legs. The body and main face are red like a ruby. The Tibetan name of Red God Cai Xing is "Ma Po Shambara", who helps poor and suffering people. It is believed that if those who have financial problems or experience any hardships in life pray to him, he will come to help them, help them escape disasters and various dangers, and experience happiness, success, and prosperity in life.

In addition, those born in the year of the dog should wear a lucky pendant of "Lord Ganesha, Success in All Things" around their neck or carry it with them when traveling near or far to make the person's fate full of auspicious treasures. There is progress in business and trade. The family is peaceful and happy throughout the year. There is better and faster efficiency and effectiveness than before.

Good Direction: Northeast, East, and South
Bad Direction: Southwest
Lucky Colors: Red, Pink, Orange, White, and Silver.
Lucky Times: 3.00 – 06.59, 11.00 – 12.59, 19.00 – 20.59.
Bad Times: 07.00 – 08.59, 13.00 – 14.59., 17.00 – 18.59

Good Luck For 2025

Made in the USA
Coppell, TX
04 January 2025

43970395R00046